THE EYES IN YOUR BODY

LAURA LORIA

Britannica®
Educational Publishing

IN ASSOCIATION WITH

ROSEN
EDUCATIONAL SERVICES

Published in 2015 by Britannica Educational Publishing (a trademark of Encyclopædia Britannica, Inc.) in association with The Rosen Publishing Group, Inc.
29 East 21st Street, New York, NY 10010

Distributed exclusively by Rosen Publishing.
To see additional Britannica Educational Publishing titles, go to rosenpublishing.com.

First Edition

Britannica Educational Publishing
J.E. Luebering: Director, Core Reference Group
Mary Rose McCudden: Editor, Britannica Student Encyclopedia

Rosen Publishing
Hope Lourie Killcoyne: Executive Editor
Jeanne Nagle: Editor
Nelson Sá: Art Director
Brian Garvey: Designer
Cindy Reiman: Photography Manager
Karen Huang: Photo Researcher

Library of Congress Cataloging-in-Publication Data

Loria, Laura, author.
The eyes in your body/Laura Loria. — First edition.
        pages cm. — (Let's find out! The human body)
Audience: Grades 3 to 6.
Includes bibliographical references and index.
ISBN 978-1-62275-648-3 (library bound) — ISBN 978-1-62275-649-0 (pbk.) —
ISBN 978-1-62275-650-6 (6-pack)
1. Eye — Juvenile literature. 2. Vision — Juvenile literature. 3. Vision disorders — Juvenile literature. I. Title.
QP475.7.L67 2015
612.8'4 — dc23
                                                                      2014022724

Manufactured in the United States of America

Photo Credits: Cover, p. 1 © iStockphoto.com/sirius r; cover, p.1 (inset) © iStockphoto.com; interior pages background © iStockphoto.com/arcoss; pp. 4-5 Netfalls-Remy Musser/Shutterstock.com; p. 5 monkeybusinessimages/iStock/Thinkstock; pp. 6-7 esra su; p. 7 Alliance/Shutterstock.com; pp. 8-9 dtimiraos/E+/Getty Images; pp. 9, 18 Encyclopædia Britannica, Inc.; pp. 10-11 Anthony Lee/Caiaimage/Getty Images; p. 11 Tim Flach/Stone/Getty Images; pp. 12, 15 BSIP/Universal Images Group/Getty Images; pp. 12-13 DEA Picture Library/De Agostini/Getty Images; p. 14 National Eye Institute, NIH; p. 16 Masson/Shutterstock.com; p. 17 FooTToo/Shutterstock.com; p. 19 Echo/Cultura/Getty Imags; p. 20 Jupiterimages/Pixland/Thinkstock; p. 21 vadim kozlovsky/Shutterstock.com; p. 22 Dmitry Naumov/Shutterstock.com; p. 23 © jackmicro/Fotolia; p. 24 Rolf Vennenbernd/dpa /Landov; p. 25 Alila Medical Media/Shutterstock.com; p. 26 Alsu/Shutterstock.com; p. 27 Jeroen van den Broek/Shutterstock.com; p. 28 Jeff Pachoud/AFP/Getty Images; p. 29 Lawrence Lawry/National Artificial Eye Service/Science Source.

CONTENTS

WHY DO WE HAVE EYES?

Human beings have five basic senses: touch, hearing, smell, taste, and sight. Different parts of the body send information to the brain about each of those senses. For sight, it is the eyes that do this work. Sight allows us to learn about the world around us and to interact with objects and people.

The eye is the organ that gives animals the ability to see.

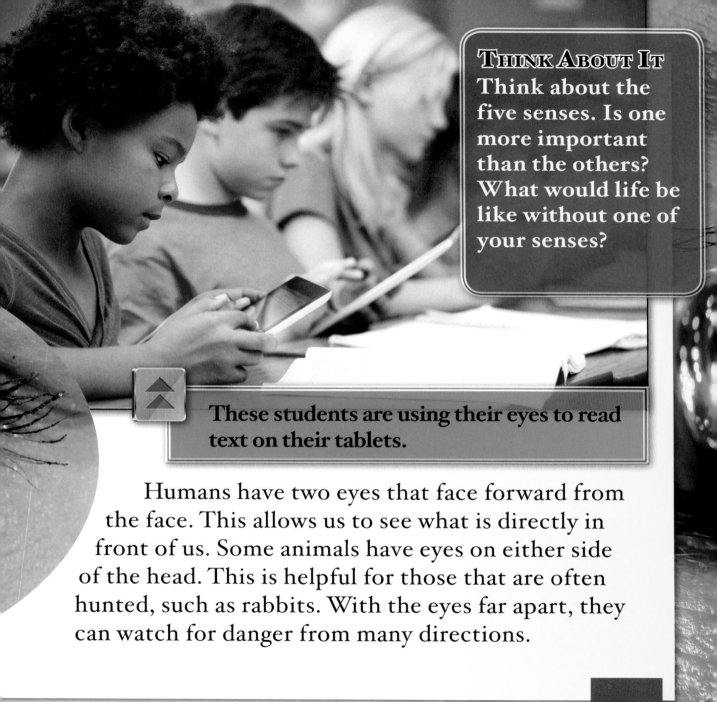

THINK ABOUT IT
Think about the five senses. Is one more important than the others? What would life be like without one of your senses?

These students are using their eyes to read text on their tablets.

Humans have two eyes that face forward from the face. This allows us to see what is directly in front of us. Some animals have eyes on either side of the head. This is helpful for those that are often hunted, such as rabbits. With the eyes far apart, they can watch for danger from many directions.

Eye Structure

Humans have two eyes. Each eye looks like a ball with a stem. The eyeball sits in a socket, or opening, in the skull. The skull bone protects the eye. The front of the eye sticks out a bit. It is protected by an eyelid.

When the eyelid closes, tears move across the eye to moisten and wash it. Eyelashes help as well.

THINK ABOUT IT

Humans blink their eyes every three or four seconds, on average. What does it feel like when you don't blink for a long time?

They act like screens on a window to keep dust and small specks of dirt out of the eyes. Eyes are filled with a clear, jellylike substance, which is surrounded by three layers. Each of these layers, called coats, contains several important parts of the eye.

Tears clear out irritations, like those caused by the oil released from chopped onions.

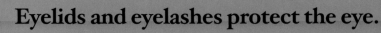

Eyelids and eyelashes protect the eye.

THE FIRST COAT

The first coat of the eye is the outer layer. It consists of parts called the sclera and the cornea. The sclera is the white part of the eye. It has a covering called a conjunctiva, which helps keep the eye from becoming dry.

The cornea is **transparent** and rounded. It rests over the center of the eye. You

An object is **transparent** when you can see clearly through it. A window is transparent.

can't see the cornea, but it is very important. The cornea is where light passes into the eye. Light is what allows us to see images. Behind the cornea is a clear, watery liquid. This liquid works with the cornea to point the light to the center of the eye.

Labels on diagram: sclera, lens, pupil, retina, optic nerve, iris, blood vessels, clear jelly, cornea

The cornea covers the exposed part of the eye.

The sclera has many small, pale pink blood vessels. When the eyes are dry or tired, the vessels grow larger and darker.

THE SECOND COAT

The second coat of the eye contains several parts, including the iris and the main blood supply for the eye.

The iris is the colored part of the eye. Eye color is different for every person. The color of your iris has nothing to do with the function of your eyes.

THINK ABOUT IT
Recall the last time you stepped outside, from a dark room to bright sunshine. What would happen if your pupils didn't change size?

The iris can be blue, green, brown, or a mixture of those colors.

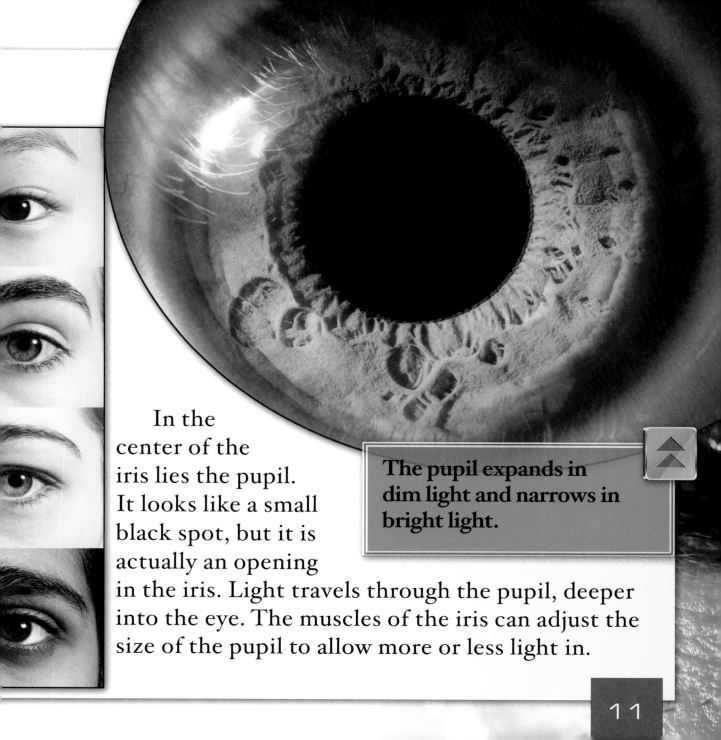

In the center of the iris lies the pupil. It looks like a small black spot, but it is actually an opening in the iris. Light travels through the pupil, deeper into the eye. The muscles of the iris can adjust the size of the pupil to allow more or less light in.

The pupil expands in dim light and narrows in bright light.

COMPARE AND CONTRAST

As people grow older, their lenses are less flexible. Do you think that older adults and school-aged children see things the same way?

The lens of the eye sits behind the iris. Like the cornea, the lens is mostly transparent and rounded. Its function is to direct light toward the back of the eye.

A clouding of the lens is known as a cataract. Cataracts can make vision blurry.

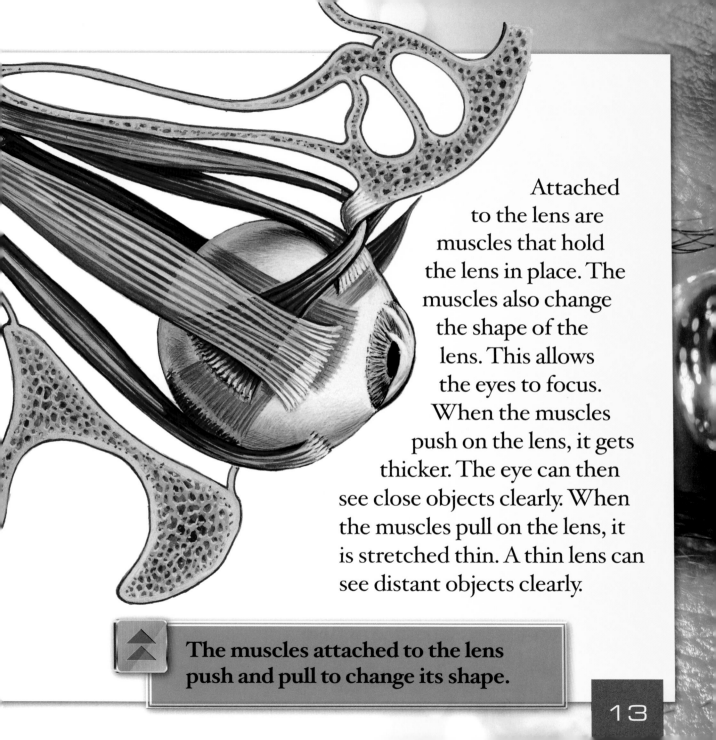

Attached to the lens are muscles that hold the lens in place. The muscles also change the shape of the lens. This allows the eyes to focus. When the muscles push on the lens, it gets thicker. The eye can then see close objects clearly. When the muscles pull on the lens, it is stretched thin. A thin lens can see distant objects clearly.

The muscles attached to the lens push and pull to change its shape.

THE THIRD COAT

The third coat is the inner layer of the eye. It is called the retina. The retina is connected to the brain through a structure called the optic nerve.

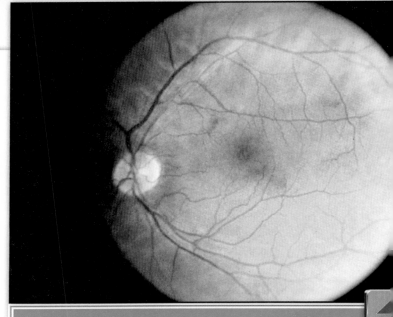

The blood vessels in the retina can be seen clearly in this image.

The retina contains millions of cells called rods and cones. These cells collect light. Chemicals in the cells convert the light they receive into electrical messages. The messages then travel through the optic nerve to the brain.

Most of the cells in the retina are rods. They can detect only black and white shapes—just the basic outline of things.

To convert something is to change it.

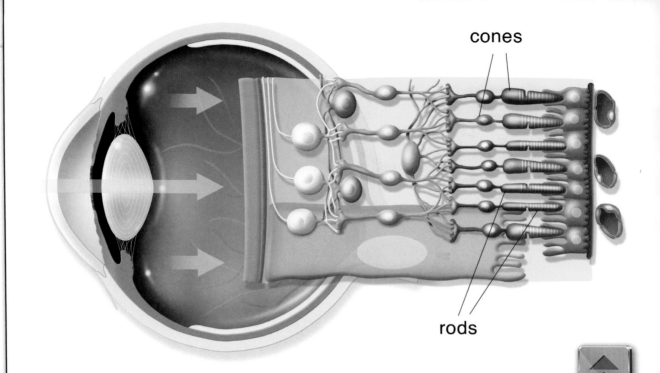

cones

rods

The cells shown to the left of the rods and cones here connect them to the optic nerve.

Cones can pick up much more detail, including color and fine lines. There are three types of cones. Each type receives a particular grouping of colors—red, green, or blue. All of the colors in the world are made of combinations of these colors.

How Do Eyes Work?

When we see an object, we actually see light reflecting, or bouncing, off that object. This light enters the eye. It passes through the cornea and the lens, which focus it toward the retina. The rods and cones in the retina change the light into

Eyes need light, whether from a lamp, a fire, or the sun, to see.

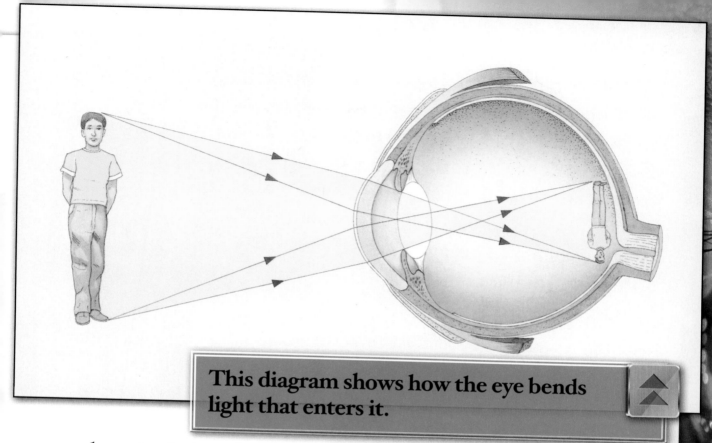

This diagram shows how the eye bends light that enters it.

electrical signals. The signals then travel to a special part of the brain.

The brain interprets these signals as an image, or picture, of the object. The eye actually receives light images upside down. One job of the brain is to flip the image over. The brain also controls the muscles in the eye that adjust the lens and the iris.

Most people use both of their eyes to receive information at the same time. Each eye sees the same thing from a slightly different angle. The brain has to use the two messages to create one complete image. This is called binocular vision.

COMPARE AND CONTRAST

Cover one of your eyes and look at an object. Then cover your other eye and look at the object again. Next, look at the object with both eyes. How does your view of the object change each time?

"Binocular" means "involving two eyes." Tools called binoculars let people see distant objects with both eyes.

The double images received by the eyes help us to see in three dimensions.

There are long muscles attached to each eyeball on the top, bottom, and sides. They control eye movement. Even though each eye has its own set of muscles, the two sets are usually able to move the eyes in the same direction at the same time.

Eye and Vision Problems

Many people have problems with their eyes. Some problems are caused by damage to the eye. Others are caused by the structure of the eye itself.

Myopia (nearsightedness)

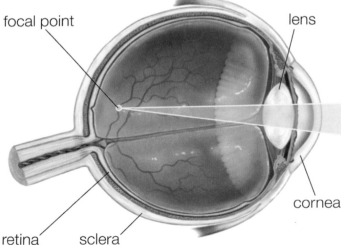

focal point · lens · cornea · retina · sclera

Normal eye

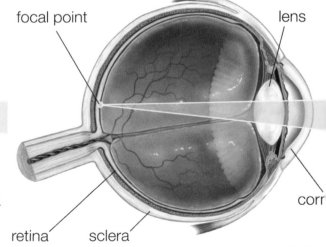

focal point · lens · corr · retina · sclera

A nearsighted eye focuses light differently than a normal eye does.

Dust or other tiny objects may get into the eye and irritate it. Eyes can also get red and swollen if they are infected with germs.

For many people, the shape of their eyes causes vision problems. When an eye is longer than usual from front to back, it is difficult for the lens to focus on objects that are far away. Those with this condition are called nearsighted. If the eye is not long enough, the lens cannot focus on objects that are close. Someone with this eye shape is called farsighted.

COMPARE AND CONTRAST

What's better or worse about being either nearsighted or farsighted?

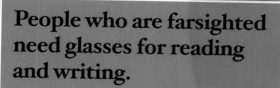

People who are farsighted need glasses for reading and writing.

21

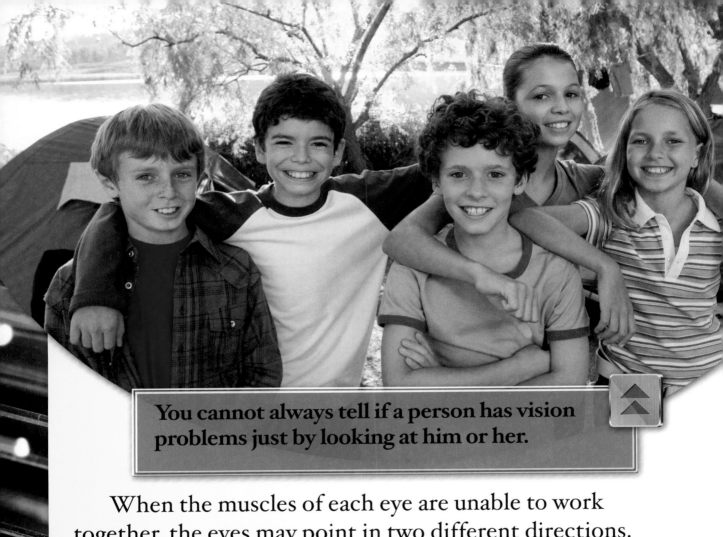

You cannot always tell if a person has vision problems just by looking at him or her.

When the muscles of each eye are unable to work together, the eyes may point in two different directions. The two separate images that are sent to the brain are too different to blend together, so a double image is produced. If the eyes point in two very different directions, the brain may use the input from only one of them to produce the image.

The cones in the retina can be damaged by disease or from an inherited condition. If that happens, then the person will have color blindness. A person with severe color blindness sees only shades of gray.

A person with red-green color blindness could not see the number in this image.

Inherited features are passed from parents to their children.

Correcting Vision Problems

How do you know if you have a vision problem? If your vision changes over time, you get headaches frequently, or your eyes feel sore, you should see an eye doctor. Eye doctors can tell which parts of your eyes are not working properly. For example, the lens in one or both of your eyes may not be focusing the light that comes into

Contact lenses work just like glasses to correct vision problems.

COMPARE AND CONTRAST

Contact lenses work the same way that glasses do. Is one better than the other?

the eye correctly. An eye doctor can order glasses to treat many vision problems. Glasses will not cure a vision problem, but they allow the wearer to see more clearly.

Glasses come in many shapes and colors.

Glasses work by bending the light coming into the eye, just as your lens is supposed to do. The glasses correct the angle of the light to allow it to focus and make a clear image. In some cases, your own lens may be removed altogether. The glasses then take the place of the lens.

Wearing glasses or contact lenses is the simplest way to correct your vision, but there are a few disadvantages. Glasses can break, scratch, slip down your nose, or feel uncomfortable at times. Contact lenses can irritate your eyes, need to be cleaned often, and can easily be lost. Some

THINK ABOUT IT
Even simple surgeries like LASIK have some risks, like permanent damage to your vision. Would you choose surgery over glasses?

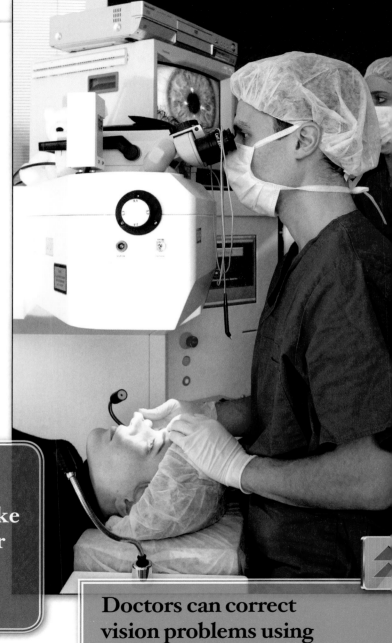
Doctors can correct vision problems using this LASIK machine.

people choose to have laser surgery to correct their vision problems.

In the past, eye surgery was performed only to correct serious vision problems. Today, many people choose a procedure called LASIK to correct their nearsightedness, farsightedness, or astigmatism. In LASIK surgery, a laser reshapes the tissues under the cornea, which changes the way light comes into the eye.

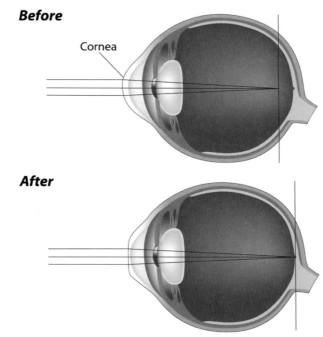

LASIK Surgery for Myopia

Before

Cornea

After

Laser surgery can correct myopia, or nearsightedness.

Blindness

A serious vision problem is called blindness. A person who is blind may not be able to see anything at all, or he or she might be able to see only simple light, colors, or shapes. Blindness can occur in one or both eyes.

There are a number of causes of blindness. Sometimes it is inherited. Other times it is due to an injury of the eyes or brain. Most often, blindness is a result of a disease

THINK ABOUT IT
How would your life change if you became blind? What would stay the same?

Braille is a code of raised dots that people read with their fingers.

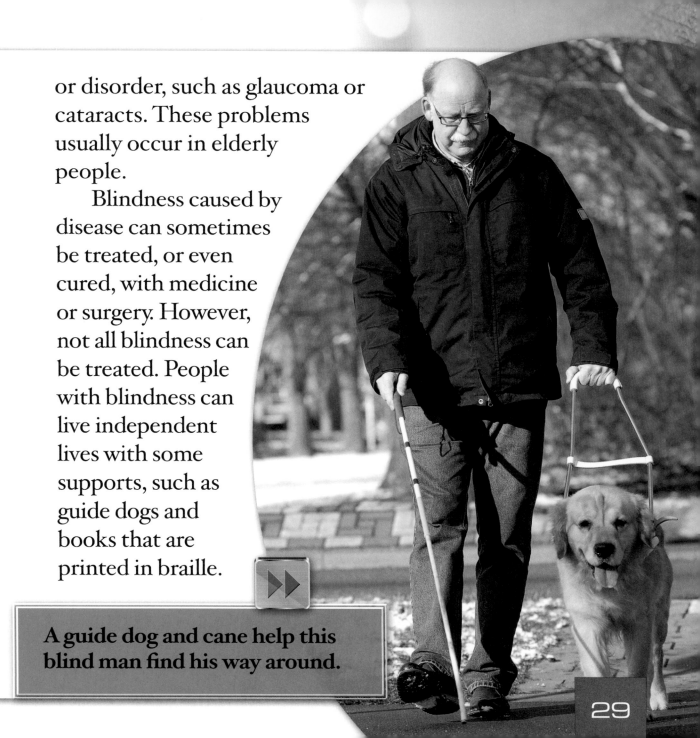

or disorder, such as glaucoma or cataracts. These problems usually occur in elderly people.

Blindness caused by disease can sometimes be treated, or even cured, with medicine or surgery. However, not all blindness can be treated. People with blindness can live independent lives with some supports, such as guide dogs and books that are printed in braille.

A guide dog and cane help this blind man find his way around.

GLOSSARY

astigmatism An eye problem that causes blurry vision.

binocular vision Seeing with both eyes at once.

braille A type of print for the blind that uses raised dots on a page.

cones Parts of the eye that can detect color and other details.

cornea The outer part of the eye, where light enters.

farsighted Trouble seeing objects that are close by.

function The special purpose or activity for which a thing exists or is used.

infected Contaminated with a disease-producing substance or agent.

iris The colored part of the eye.

irritate To make (a part of the body) sore or painful.

lens The part of the eye that brings objects into focus.

nearsighted Trouble seeing objects that are far away.

pupil The black dot in the middle of the eye that adjusts to light.

retina The part of the eye that turns light into electrical messages for the brain.

socket An opening that holds something.

For More Information

Books

Ballard, Carol. *How Your Eyes Work*. New York, NY: Gareth Stevens, 2010.

Caster, Shannon. *Eyes*. New York, NY: PowerKids Press, 2010.

Macaulay, David. *Eye: How It Works*. New York, NY: David Macaulay Studio, 2013.

Silke, Janet. *Take a Closer Look at Your Eyes*. North Mankato, MN: Child's World, 2013.

Stewart, Melissa. *The Eyes Have It: The Secrets of Eyes and Seeing*. Tarrytown, NY: Benchmark Books, 2009.

Websites

Because of the changing nature of Internet links, Rosen Publishing has developed an online list of websites related to the subject of this book. This site is updated regularly. Please use this link to access the list:

http://www.rosenlinks.com/LFO/Eyes

INDEX